A CourseGuide for

# Cultural
# Apologetics

# Paul M. Gould

ZONDERVAN
ACADEMIC

ZONDERVAN ACADEMIC

*A CourseGuide for Cultural Apologetics*
Copyright © 2020 by Zondervan

Requests for information should be addressed to:
Zondervan, *3900 Sparks Dr. SE, Grand Rapids, Michigan 49546*

ISBN 978-0-310-11048-4 (softcover)

*Printed in the United States of America*

# CONTENTS

# Introduction

Welcome to the *A CourseGuide for Cultural Apologetics*. These guides were created for formal and informal students alike who want to engage deeper in biblical, theological, or ministry studies. We hope this guide will provide an opportunity for you to grow not only in your understanding, but also in your faith.

## How to Use This Guide

This guide is meant to be used in conjunction with the book *Cultural Apologetics* and its corresponding videos, *Cultural Apologetics Video Lectures*. After you have read each chapter in the book and watched the accompanying video lesson, the materials in this guide will help you review and assess what you have learned. Application-oriented questions are included as well.

Each CourseGuide has been individually designed to best equip you in your studies, but in general, you can expect the following components. Most CourseGuides begin every chapter with a "You Should Know" section, which highlights key terminology, people, and facts to remember. This section serves as a helpful summary for directing your studies. Reflection questions, typically two to three per chapter, prompt you to summarize key points you've learned. Discussion questions invite you to an even deeper level of engagement. Finally, most chapters will end with a short quiz to test your retention. You can find the answer key to each quiz at the bottom of the page following it.

## For Further Study

CourseGuides accompany books and videos from some of the world's top biblical and theological scholars. They may be used independently, or in small groups or classrooms, offering quality instruction to equip students for academic and ministry pursuits. If you would like to engage in further study with Zondervan's CourseGuides, the full lineup may be viewed online. After completing your studies with *A CourseGuide for Cultural Apologetics*, we recommend moving on to *A CourseGuide for Tactics: A Game Plan for Discussing Your Christian Convictions* and *A CourseGuide for Evangelism in a Skeptical World*.

# CHAPTER 1

# What Is Cultural Apologetics?

## You Should Know

- The three elements of "Our Athens": disenchanted, sensate, hedonistic

- Reason guides us on the quest for truth. The conscience leads us to goodness. And the imagination transports us toward beauty. This is also why we have intellectuals, prophets, and artists. They can perform a priestly duty, leading us if we allow them toward the ultimate object of our soul's longing: Jesus Christ, the source of all truth, goodness, and beauty.

- If a genuine missionary encounter between Christianity and Western culture were to happen, and the church could bridge the gap by pointing to the truth, goodness, and beauty the culture longs for, I believe it would lead to the reestablishment of the Christian imagination, mind, and conscience.

- The gospel no longer receives a fair hearing (the Christian voice is muted). Christians find themselves as morally fragmented as their non-Christian neighbors (the Christian conscience is muted). The collective imagination of Christian culture is focused on the mundane (the Christian imagination is muted).

- Berger says every culture has a collective mind-set, a collective imagination, and a collective conscience. This combined outlook shapes the culture's view of the world and what is judged within the culture as plausible or implausible. Is this a genuine possibility . . . or just an outrageous idea?

- Sensate: a cultural mode of thinking fixated on the physical, the sensory, and the material

- Plausibility structure: the collective mind-set, collective imagination, and collective conscience of a culture

- Traditional apologetics: the discipline concerned with making arguments to defend Christian truth claims and that has often addressed challenges to Christian belief coming from philosophical and more intellectual sources

- Cultural apologetics: the work of establishing the Christian voice, conscience, and imagination within a culture so that Christianity is seen as true and satisfying

- Rational apologetics: the approach to apologetics that begins with (or focuses primarily on) reason

## Essay Questions

### Short

1. Explain the difference between traditional and cultural apologetics. Use at least one well-developed example to explain the distinction.

2. What is Gould's account of the relationship between Christianity and contemporary human culture? Why do you think Christianity seems irrelevant to some in your contemporary culture? What might you say to "resurrect the relevance" of Christianity for such people?

3. Explain, using examples, the statement: "A missionary encounter requires Christians to engage both 'upstream' within these centers of cultural influence and 'downstream' where culture is largely consumed." How might this look to engage this way in your contemporary culture?

### Long

1. Gould argues that modern Western culture ("Our Athens") is "disenchanted, sensate, and hedonistic." What does he mean by each of these

aspects of culture? Describe his view using concrete examples, and then describe what an unbelieving Westerner might say as an objection to his claim. If the objection seems ineffective to you, respond on behalf of Gould.

## Quiz

1. According to Gould, what is the "question that drives the work of cultural apologetics"?
    a) Where can the gospel gain a foothold in our culture?
    b) Which cultural medium communicates the gospel most readily?
    c) How can we have a genuine missionary encounter in our culture?
    d) Which is the best argument for God's existence in our culture?

2. Gould defines "cultural apologetics" as the work of establishing the Christian voice, conscience, and imagination within a culture so that Christianity is seen as _____ and _____.
    a) Beautiful, good
    b) Fun, exciting
    c) True, satisfying
    d) Rational, unchanging

3. Since the Enlightenment, apologetics has primarily been conceived as a defense of the _____ of Christianity.
    a) Reasonableness
    b) Truth
    c) Superiority
    d) Principles

4. The approach to apologetics that begins with (or focuses primarily on) the human conscience is classified as _____.
    a) Imaginative apologetics
    b) Moral apologetics
    c) Sapiential apologetics
    d) Popologetics

5. What is the key term used to describe the way modern Western culture perceives the world?

   a) Jaded
   b) Bored
   c) Captivated
   d) Disenchanted

6. What key term is used to describe the way people in the modern Western culture think?

   a) Materialistic
   b) Mundane
   c) Sensate
   d) Illogical

7. What term is used to describe the way people in modern Western culture live?

   a) Hedonistic
   b) Amoral
   c) Eudemonistic
   d) Self-centered

8. Gould thinks the Christian virtues of faith, hope, and love have been replaced by three modern virtues. What are they?

   a) Courage, tolerance, justice
   b) Tolerance, personal autonomy, progressivism
   c) Justice, peace, personal autonomy
   d) Pleasure, liberalism, tolerance

9. One "tragedy of the fall is the loss of _____."

   a) Beauty
   b) Morality
   c) Truth
   d) Paradise

10. Christians ought to view Jesus as an authority not only on spiritual and moral matters, but also on matters related to _____.

   a) Family dynamics
   b) Material possessions
   c) The acquisition of knowledge
   d) Business relationships

# CHAPTER 2

# Disenchantment

## You Should Know

- God reveals himself to us because he wants us to flourish.

- The elements of biblical "Exitus-Reditus": God, Wander, Turning Point, Return

- While philosophers, theologians, and historians disagree over the details, they tend to agree that the unraveling of what Hans Boersma calls the 'sacramental tapestry' of the world can be traced to at least three philosophical ideas: nominalism, mechanism, and empiricism.

- The goal of life in our modern culture is no longer virtue oriented toward an end (as the Greeks argued) or religion oriented toward the divine (as the medievals argued). Rather, the goal of life is entirely subjective. It is found within the *self*. To be specific, the defining goal of an individual's life in this disenchanted age is the satisfaction of their personal desires.

- In a disenchanted age belief in God is unwelcome, unnecessary, and unimaginable.

- The architects of our disenchantment have created a genuine mess. Human beings were not meant to live like cattle, and a life solely focused on sensual experience will never satisfy us. And those who become disillusioned with the ho-hum manna provided by modernity will end up in a state of despair.

- Peter Berger points to five "signals" of transcendence from our everyday experiences: (1) the human propensity for order; (2) the pervasiveness of human play; (3) the unconquerable human propensity to hope; (4) in the face of horrendous evil, the human demand for damnation; and (5) the reality of humor. Possible distractors:

- Manicheism: a pagan cult that believed God and evil were two equal forces dueling for the fate of the world

- Naturalism: the view that there is nothing beyond nature

- Materialism: the view that there is nothing more to reality than the material

- A model for re-enchantment:

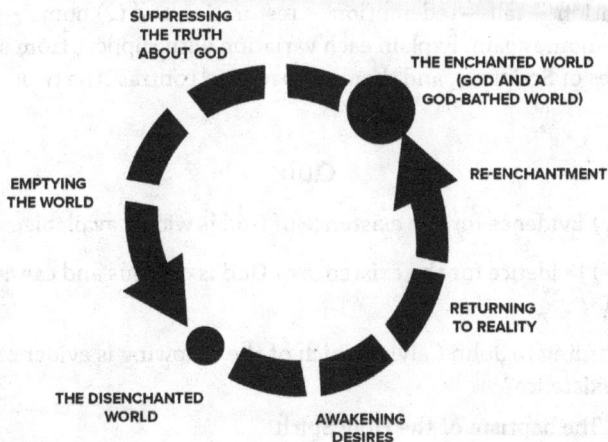

FIGURE 2.2 A MODEL FOR RE-ENCHANTMENT

# Essay Questions

## *Short*

1. What is it to perceive the world in "disenchanted" and "enchanted" ways? Explain and contrast the concepts.

2. Choose an aspect of your life—a person, a relationship, an object, an experience, etc.—with respect to which you have experienced C. S. Lewis's four stages of enchantment. For that aspect of your life, explain each stage and how you transitioned between them. (p. 43–44)

3. Explain three signs of "disenchantment" that you see in both contemporary culture and the Christian church. If possible, use examples from your own life or church.

### Long

1. This section presents two variations on the plotline of Scripture: (1) creation — fall — redemption — restoration and (2) home — away — home again. Explain each variation with support from specific passages of Scripture, and then compare and contrast the two.

## Quiz

1. (T/F) Evidence for the existence of God is widely available.

2. (T/F) Evidence for the existence of God is obvious and cannot be missed.

3. According to John Calvin, which of the following is evidence of God's existence?

    a) The baptism of the Holy Spirit
    b) The rightness and wrongness of certain actions
    c) The workmanship of the universe
    d) The definition of the concept "God"

4. Which of the following is NOT something listed as a helpful guide to reenchantment of our perception of the world?

    a) The story of Scripture
    b) Popular culture
    c) Saint Augustine
    d) Dallas Willard

5. Which of the following is NOT an element in the portrayal of biblical "exitus-reditus"?

  a) Wander
  b) God
  c) Return
  d) Celebration

6. Which of the following steps toward disenchantment is explicitly associated with idolatry?

  a) Suppressing the truth about God
  b) The disenchanted world
  c) Emptying the world
  d) Rejecting the Spirit

7. Disenchantment is marked by four key characteristics. What are they?

  a) A compromised morality, worship of money, blindness and foolishness, and patent injustice
  b) The felt absence of God, a consumer culture, blindness and foolishness, and idolatry
  c) Self-centeredness, a consumer culture, family breakdown, and idolatry
  d) A compromised morality, family breakdown, a consumer culture, and patent injustice

8. What are the four traditional arguments for the existence of God?

  a) Ontological, cosmological, teleological, and moral
  b) Experiential, bimodal, ontological, and theological
  c) Bimodal, experiential, teleological, and cosmological
  d) Ethereal, theological, moral, and ontological

9. Staunch atheist Richard Dawkins thinks that "appeals to God shut down the process of _____."

  a) Becoming an adult
  b) Imagination
  c) Gaining knowledge
  d) Spiritual growth

10. Norman Wirzba states that "the naming and narrating of the world is no trivial thing . . . because the way we name and narrate the world [and ourselves] _____."

   a) Makes up the lens through which we see it
   b) Has the power to build up or destroy
   c) Is either carnal or spiritual
   d) Determines how we are going to live in it

# CHAPTER 3

# Reenchantment

## You Should Know

- Our most fundamental mode of orientation to the world is love. We are oriented by our longings, directed by our desires.

- Sloth's main target is our love relationship with God, in the context of a life in which we take our likeness to God to be our defining identity and loving communion with God to be our main vocation as human beings.

- There are at least three ways we can join with the Holy Spirit in awakening desire in those we seek to reach with the gospel: the way of imagination, the way of reason, and the way of morality.

- The premises and conclusion of the "Argument from Desire": our natural desires have a corresponding object that satisfies them; there exists in us a natural desire, the desire for transcendence, that nothing in the material cosmos can satisfy; there exists some object beyond the material cosmos that can satisfy this desire; the transcendent object of our longing is God; God exists

- For Jesus, nothing is mundane. The world is God-bathed, full of wonder and delight. The world is God permeated. God does not exist in some unreachable domain separated from earth by vast, empty space. God is an ever-present reality.

- How Paul and Barnabas respond to people they encounter in Lystra in Acts 14: Paul and Barnabas implore the people to stop worshiping them; Paul points to the world and then claims that God is its Creator; Paul draws attention to the good things God has given his creatures; Paul implores them to see God as the giver of these good things

- Neopaganism is a false reenchantment because it does not evoke the pleasure of a dream, but that of a nightmare, where we are trapped in a world that is magical, but not good.

- Returning to reality: (1) seeing and delighting in reality in the same way that Jesus sees and delights in reality and (2) inviting others to see and delight in reality in the same way

- Materialism: the view that only matter and the material cosmos exist

- Contemporary humanism: a "here and now" transcendence according to which reality is transcendent because there are things that exist in this world that are beyond our ability to comprehend

- Trans/post-humanism: the view that technology will allow us to transcend the intellectual, psychological, and physical limitations of human existence

## Essay Questions
### Short

1. "Cultural apologetics involves drawing attention to this universal longing for happiness and the fruitless efforts of humanity to attain happiness through self-effort or created things." Explain two examples of fruitless efforts to attain happiness in your culture. How can directing attention to the longing for happiness draw people to God?

2. "Cultural apologetics involves cultivating spiritual perception, recognizing that creation itself offers glimpses of the divine." Explain at least two ways in which we might cultivate this "spiritual perception." (p. 83–84)

3. Explain Luc Ferry's "contemporary humanism" in your own words. What's wrong with Ferry's view? Explain an objection to it.

### Long

1. Analyze the apostle Paul's proclamation in Acts 14:12–17 as what Gould calls "a model for helping others return to reality." What is

Gould's account of how Paul calls his hearers to reality? What parts of Paul's proclamation do you view as most useful in your current cultural context? Are there any aspects of Paul's proclamation that you think would not be useful today? Explain.

## Quiz

1. According to Gould, we are _____ animals.

    a) Carnal
    b) Instinctive
    c) Desiring
    d) Terrified

2. Traditionally, love has been understood as a _____.

    a) Cardinal virtue
    b) Theological virtue
    c) Habit
    d) Central attitude

3. The process of reenchantment begins with _____.

    a) Reawakening innate desires
    b) Becoming convinced of God's existence
    c) Encountering God's Word
    d) Accepting Jesus as Lord and Savior

4. "The strongest objection to the argument from desire comes from the field of _____."

    a) Anthropology
    b) Philosophy
    c) Evolutionary psychology
    d) Linguistics

5. The second step on the path to reenchantment is _____.

    a) The awakening of desire
    b) Abandonment of sin
    c) A conversion of the mind
    d) A return to reality

6. The calling of Christians is to be curators of culture in the hope that Christianity will be seen as _____ and _____.

    a) Feasible, strong
    b) Plausible, desirable
    c) Joyful, peaceful
    d) Just, true

7. By perceiving the world as enchanted, we _____ it and find _____ in it too.

    a) Savor, sustenance
    b) Study, great curiosity
    c) Embrace, comfort
    d) Evaluate, evil

8. Which of the following is not one of the "three false enchantments" that are especially appealing in contemporary Western culture?

    a) Contemporary humanism
    b) Augmented and virtual realities
    c) Manicheism
    d) Neopaganism

9. Which of the following is a problem with augmented and virtual realities?

    a) They remove us from the real world
    b) They are too expensive
    c) They inhibit our relationships with other people
    d) They are environmentally unsustainable

10. Which of the following is Gould's definition of neopaganism?

    a) A new religion according to which every material object is divine
    b) A new spiritual movement that is materialistic, pluralist, and transcendental
    c) A new religious practice involving worship of plants and animals
    d) A new spiritualism that is often atheistic, individualistic, and experiential

ANSWER KEY
1. C, 2. B, 3. A, 4. C, 5. D, 6. B, 7. A, 8. C, 9. A, 10. D

# CHAPTER 4

# Imagination

## You Should Know

- Stories move the heart. Beauty awakens our longings, and the imagination paints pictures in our mind that help us see reality more clearly.

- Three observations about Exodus 31:1–11: (1) there are artists in the community of Israel; (2) God calls the artists by name and fills them with his Spirit to accomplish their task; (3) God calls the artists to make artistic things

- Art is not meant to be an *object* of worship; it is an *aid* to worship. We can go a step further, however. God is the master artist: it is *his* pattern for the tabernacle, and it is *our* home he creates and cultivates in the opening chapters of Genesis.

- Regardless of our own artistic ability (or lack thereof), Christians are called to be creators and cultivators of the good, true, and beautiful. Andy Crouch says that we express our God-given humanity as creative cultivators through the *things* and *meaning* we make of the world. As artists and gardeners, we do this by *bringing beauty back into our lives and into the church.*

- Two characteristics must an activity possess in order to be a *creative* activity: (1) novelty and (2) value

- As cultural apologists, our task is to demonstrate that the best explanation for why we make architecture and jokes, sculptures and gardens, stories and mythical creatures is because we bear the image of a God who is the master creator, comedian, and storyteller.

- Gould's working definition of imagination: a faculty of the mind that mediates between sense and intellect (i.e., perception and reason) and the human mind and the divine mind (i.e., finite creatures and the infinite Creator) for meaning and inventing

- Subjectivism about beauty: the view that judgments of beauty are subjective and not objective

- *Homo imaginans*: the one who imagines

- The Human Quest for Beauty:

**FIGURE 4.1: THE HUMAN QUEST FOR BEAUTY**

## Essay Questions

### Short

1. "As God's image bearers, we are called to be artists and gardeners after his image." Is there a form of art or gardening that you are drawn to practice? What is it? If you are currently practicing it, how did you come to do so, and what is your practice? If you are not currently practicing it, what are some steps you could take toward practicing it?

2. Timothy Keller provocatively suggests that the church can neither praise God nor reach the world without art. Using examples, explain how this could be.

3. Reflect theologically on the portrait of Frankenstein and his creature in Mary Shelley's novel. What does the story suggest to you about human creativity? About God's relationship to humans? Our attitudes toward God?

### Long

1. Gould claims that the church generally lacks a theology of beauty. Why is this? Now, make a start on developing such a theology. What exactly is beauty? How is it related to God and human beings? What is the purpose of beauty in God's economy? Explain your answers in reference to relevant passages of Scripture.

### Quiz

1. Art has a unique capacity to do which of the following?

   a) Move the heart
   b) Bypass our defenses
   c) Touch our identity
   d) All of the above

2. Why is the philistinism of contemporary art a problem for the church?

   a) Because it leads Christians to abandon the quest for beauty
   b) Because it corrupts the mind of Christians
   c) Because it distorts the gospel
   d) Because it is inspired by demonic powers

3. What did the Israelites need most?

   a) Manna
   b) Beauty
   c) God's presence
   d) To reject idolatry

4. What is the main scriptural parallel for the tabernacle?

    a) The garden of Eden

    b) Solomon's temple

    c) The city of Jerusalem

    d) Jesus's body

5. Artists help us to ___, ___, and ___ reality as it is.

    a) Hide from, dare to explore, rediscover

    b) Escape, forget, remember

    c) Fear, love, embrace

    d) See, understand, enjoy

6. What is the relationship between beauty and the mundane?

    a) Beauty *is* the mundane, only glorified.

    b) Beauty and the mundane are often juxtaposed.

    c) Beauty transports us out of the mundane.

    d) Beauty becomes mundane in the fallen world.

7. Which of the following is NOT mentioned as one of the tools through which we make sense of God, our lives, and the world?

    a) Metaphor

    b) Story

    c) Instinct

    d) Language

8. "In invention the human imagination partakes of ____."

    a) Rationality

    b) The divine

    c) The human essence

    d) God's provision

9. "Stories help 'clean our windows' so that we see the familiar in its proper light as ____."

    a) Beautiful, mysterious, and sacred

    b) Mundane, ordinary, yet good

    c) Known, comfortable, and encouraging

    d) Sinful, dark, and troubling

10. "Many, if not all, good stories are good *precisely because* _____."

a) They show us the great variety of people in the world

b) They teach us the truth about an important issue

c) They give us an appreciation for different personalities and social customs

d) They point to the one true story of the world: the gospel

# CHAPTER 5

# Reason

## You Should Know

- Over the past several decades we've witnessed the dumbing down of the Western mind. With the advent of the information age and the ubiquity of image, video, and the internet, our brains themselves are changing, and not for the better. Studies have demonstrated that we are losing our minds.

- As Francis Bacon said, God has given us two books as sources of truth: the book of God's works (creation) and the book of God's word (the Bible). Scripture implores us to study both books.

- Suppose your new gay friend has recently expressed curiosity about Christianity and your faith. At a party, he asks you what, exactly, is so special about Jesus. Tell your friend that Jesus died on the cross for the sin of the world and rose from the dead to inaugurate a New Age of redemption and transformation.

- New Atheists: a group of especially bold and confident contemporary opponents of theism, including Richard Dawkins, Christopher Hitchens, and Sam Harris

- Scientism: the view that science is the sole means of attaining knowledge

- Basic belief: a belief that is justified (and rational) in virtue of experience

- Mental causation: the causing of one mental state by another mental state

- Logical laws: laws that specify the truth-preserving relationships among propositions

- Sacred core: the set of values or beliefs cherished by members of a particular community

- The Human Quest for Truth:

FIGURE 5.1 THE HUMAN QUEST FOR TRUTH

- The Human Quest for Goodness:

FIGURE 6:1: THE HUMAN QUEST FOR GOODNESS

## Essay Questions

### Short

1. Gould mentions in passing several atheistic challenges to Christian faith. As best you can from Gould's references, explain the challenge that most worries you, and how you might begin to respond to the challenge.

2. What do Romans 12:2 and 1 Peter 3:15 teach us about reason? Explain the components of the process of using our reason to arrive at truth. Use examples to clarify each component.

3. According to Aristotle, "the credibility of our message (*logos*) is influenced by who we are (*ethos*)." Explain what this means, using examples, and what role in an argument this might play.

### Long

1. Describe the "plausibility structure" and "sacred core" of contemporary Western culture. Which elements stand most in the way of acceptance of the gospel? In light of these obstacles, explain how you might go about sharing the gospel with a contemporary Westerner. What would you say? What would you *not* say?

## Quiz

1. Christians may unwittingly contribute to the view that their faith is irrational by "seeing their own faith _____."

    a) In experiential or emotional categories
    b) As not grounded in reasons
    c) As a "leap in the dark"
    d) As blind

2. C. S. Lewis claimed, "One of the things that distinguishes man from other animals is that he wants to know things, wants to find out what reality is like, _____."

    a) In order to promote his happiness
    b) As a means of survival

    c) So as to feel secure in the world

    d) Simply for the sake of knowing

3. Why is Isaac Watts a helpful example of a cultural apologist?

    a) Because Watts was an extraordinary musician

    b) Because Watts composed several famous hymns

    c) Because Watts embodied commitments both to God and to good reasoning

    d) Because Watts published a famous textbook on logic

4. What is an "inferential belief"?

    a) A belief that a certain logical inference is valid

    b) A belief arrived at by logical inference from two other propositions

    c) A belief arrived at by immediate perception

    d) A belief grounded in a kind of rational seeming

5. Which of the following is NOT a claim that a naturalist is committed to?

    a) There is nothing that is divine, or sacred, or worthy of worship.

    b) There are none but natural causes involving none but natural entities.

    c) Nature is important and should be preserved.

    d) The distribution of minds in the universe is late and local.

6. "If theism is true, . . . mind is both _____ matter and _____ matter. Mental causation fits nicely within a theistic framework."

    a) Prior to, the cause of

    b) Over, under

    c) Within, beyond

    d) Caused by, after

7. A statement or proposition is necessarily true if _____.

    a) It is physically true

    b) It could be false

    c) It is possibly true

    d) It could not be false

8. The statement, "The Union won the Civil War" is a contingent truth because _____.

    a) It is historically true
    b) It could have been false
    c) It could not be false
    d) It is necessary

9. If the premises are true, in which kind of argument does the conclusion probably (but not inescapably) follow?

    a) Deductive
    b) Modus ponens
    c) Inductive
    d) Disjunctive syllogism

10. According to Gould, the chief sins of our disenchanted age are _____.

    a) Racism and sexism
    b) Homophobia and prudishness
    c) Economic injustice and emotional insensitivity
    d) Hypocrisy and judgmentalism

# CHAPTER 6

# Conscience

## You Should Know

- Three aspects of a good human life: (1) right relation within ourselves; (2) right relations to others; (3) right relation to our end

- Three aspects of the human quest for goodness: (1) wholeness; (2) justice; (3) significance

- Why does God allow pain and suffering? This is one of the most common questions people ask to express their doubts about God. It is a question driven by an intuition that something has gone terribly wrong with the world.

- The premises and conclusion of C. S. Lewis's "Argument from Morality": there is a universal moral law; if there is a universal moral law, there is a moral lawgiver; if there is a moral lawgiver, it must be something beyond the material cosmos; therefore, there is something beyond the material cosmos

- According to Mark Linville, what grounds the intrinsic value of persons is the personhood of God.

- It is awe-inspiring to think that there is an absolute goodness, a power beyond the universe that presses itself within the universe. But it is equally tragic, for we fall woefully short of the moral law every day. This is the beginning of the gospel story.

- Moral law: the law of right behavior

- Moral realism: the view that there are objective moral facts (e.g., values and duties)

- Platonic atheism: the view that God does not exist, but that objective moral values do exist

- Emotivism: the view that moral claims are merely expressions of emotion

## Essay Questions

### Short

1. Of the three aspects of a good life mentioned, choose the two aspects that you find most challenging to enact. Explain what makes them challenging for you and what you might do to take a step toward achieving them.

2. Explain in your own words the view that the Trinity serves as a pattern for human wholeness.

3. "If naturalism is true and there is no transcendent reality, then there is no objective justice or actual obligation to others. It's just an illusion created by chemicals, a self-imposed obligation." Imagine and explain how an atheist who believes in objective morality might respond to this claim. If you think the response is inadequate, offer a counter-argument to it.

### Long

1. What do you think is the best explanation of the existence of the moral law, and why do you think this? Make an argument for your view and defend it from likely objections.

## Quiz

1. (T/F) Living a good life is solely about cultivating individual intellectual and moral virtue.

2. (T/F) The Trinity is a pattern for human wholeness.

3. What is the goal or purpose of human life?

   a) To achieve happiness
   b) To imitate Jesus
   c) To love and serve God
   d) To obey divine law

4. "The question of why God allows evil reveals a deep human longing for _____."

   a) Wholeness
   b) A world made right
   c) Moral beauty
   d) Truth

5. W. H. Auden's experience of evil conflicted with which of the following?

   a) His belief that humans are naturally good
   b) His belief that there are no moral absolutes
   c) His rejection of Christianity
   d) All of the above

6. Bill and Melinda Gates, Warren Buffett, Mark Zuckerberg, and Priscilla Chan exemplify the human desire for ____.

   a) Wealth
   b) Power
   c) Significance
   d) Justice

7. One reason naturalistic strategies for grounding morality fail is that _____.

   a) They have no role for God
   b) They fail to secure the objectivity of morality
   c) Natural facts and moral facts are different in kind
   d) Such strategies ignore logical facts

8. According to Gould, the only genuine candidates for transcendent objects that explain the moral law are either a _____ or _____ mind.

   a) Personal, impersonal
   b) Rational, non-rational

c) Deliberative, instinctive
d) Finite, infinite

9. According to C. S. Lewis, the source of morality ____ the universe and is the ____ behind the moral law.

a) Governs, power
b) Created, creativity
c) Is outside, intelligence
d) Watches over, enforcer

10. Which of the following is NOT one of the "greatest obstacles to the reception of the gospel" mentioned?

a) False ideas
b) Disordered loves
c) Disenchanted imaginations
d) Corrupt consciences

# CHAPTER 7

# Addressing Barriers

## You Should Know

- Christians today no longer know how to make informed decisions. Guided by raw and untutored emotion instead of reason, image instead of argument, the church is vulnerable to the ever-changing whims of a culture charting a course through a disenchanted abyss.

- Steps to recovering the Christian intellect: (1) gaining an accurate view of Jesus; (2) viewing study as part of our apprenticeship to Christ

- Three aspects of human flourishing identified by Miroslav Volf: (1) the active dimension (life being led well); (2) the passive dimension (life going well); (3) the affective dimension (life feeling good)

- Four beliefs in Western culture that, if true, either refute Christianity or require Christians to significantly modify or jettison tradition: (1) science disproves God; (2) belief in Jesus as the one and only God is intolerant; (3) God is not good; (4) Christianity offers an archaic, repressive, and unloving ethic

- Three theodicies discussed by Gould: (1) the free will theodicy; (2) the soul-making theodicy; (3) the greater-goods theodicy

- Passive nihilism: the approach to life whereby one seeks supernatural bliss while passing over life's ordinary pleasures

- Active nihilism: the approach to life whereby one defines one's own values and lives according to them

- Sacramental view of reality: the view that everything is sacred and interconnected

- Scientism: the view that science is the only or best source of knowledge

- Theodicy: a God-justifying reason for evil

## Essay Questions

### Short

1. Where do you see evidence of anti-intellectualism in the contemporary church? Explain two examples. What makes them anti-intellectual?

2. Gould mentions a number of disciplines that he believes will transform our imagination and way of seeing the world, if practiced regularly. Describe these disciplines. Which of the disciplines do you practice? Are there any that you would like to add to your repertoire? Describe a plan to put them into action.

3. Some skeptics object that Christianity's exclusive truth claims (e.g., that Jesus is the only way to God) are intolerant, and thus intellectually and morally deficient. Explain this skeptical view and the reasons some skeptics see for holding it. Then, respond to the objection.

### Long

1. Explain in your own words the account of the fragmentation of life in contemporary Western culture and a suggested path to wholeness. Use examples to clarify your explanation. Then, raise an objection to this suggestion and how you might respond.

## Quiz

1. Recovery of the Christian intellect requires that we come to see Jesus as _____. (p. 214)

    a) Beautiful
    b) Loving
    c) Brilliant
    d) Kind

2. Many contemporary Westerners live a fragmented existence, caught between our longings for _____ and _____.

    a) Meaning, pleasure
    b) Beauty, utility
    c) Significance, comfort
    d) Love, autonomy

3. Which of the following is NOT one of the beliefs Charles Taylor highlights as informing the collective imagination of European culture in the medieval period?

    a) Earthly kingdoms reflect the kingdom of God
    b) The natural world is a signpost, pointing beyond itself to God
    c) People live in an enchanted world
    d) Human character is fixed and determined by lineage

4. In order to reclaim a sacramental view of reality, "right beliefs are needed, but we also need _____ rooted in a larger narrative that can shape and renew our imagination."

    a) Feelings and emotions
    b) Practices and habits
    c) Desires and longings
    d) Creativity and action

5. Which of the following are disciplines of encountering God and opening us to spiritual formation?

    a) Worship with the church
    b) Daily Scripture reading
    c) Service to others
    d) All of the above

6. Alex Rosenberg writes, "We trust science as the only way to _____. That is why we are so confident about atheism."

    a) Disprove the existence of God
    b) Acquire knowledge
    c) Make arguments
    d) Study the universe

7. "Atheism does not give us good news; it gives us a bad story."
Which of the following is NOT a reason atheism gives us a bad story?

    a) The story does not offer hope
    b) The story does not understand our innate human longings
    c) The story has no climax or resolution
    d) The story does not understand our innate human dreams

8. Which theodicy holds that "God uses pain and suffering to grow our character"?

    a) The free will theodicy
    b) The greater goods theodicy
    c) The virtue theodicy
    d) The soul-making theodicy

9. "Skeptical theists" hold that ____.

    a) Human limitations often prohibit us from discerning God's reason for allowing evil
    b) God doesn't really care about the suffering of human beings
    c) God exists but that the Bible is not God's written Word
    d) God exists but that we can't know anything else about God

10. According to the philosopher Peter Kreeft, "We ought to be egalitarian with ____ and elitist with ____."

    a) Christians, non-Christians
    b) Non-Christians, Christians
    c) People, ideas
    d) Ideas, people

# CHAPTER 8

# Home

## You Should Know

- Whether we're rich or poor, male or female . . . our stories are all stories of searching.

- In short, home is an apt metaphor for our hearts' deepest longings — for God, wholeness, meaning, and purpose; a place and path where life is experienced as it was meant to be.

- Gould reminds us that the story of Genesis 3 accounts for the human condition of homelessness.

- In Christ, life is full of paradox. We die in order to live. We seek another to find ourselves. We gain the whole world but lose our soul. In the end, you will either save your life by giving it away or lose it by trying to save it yourself; you will either find the happiness and home that God gives and enjoy it in creaturely response or eternally starve.

- The three elements of the major plotline in the story of naturalism: matter, ignorance, progress

- The three elements of the major plotline in the story of postmodernism: culture, oppression, expression

- What makes the Christian story a "fairy story" is the fact that the story continues with eternal happiness.

- Home: a place to stand and a story in which to live

- *Shalom*: universal flourishing, wholeness, and delight

- The Journey Home

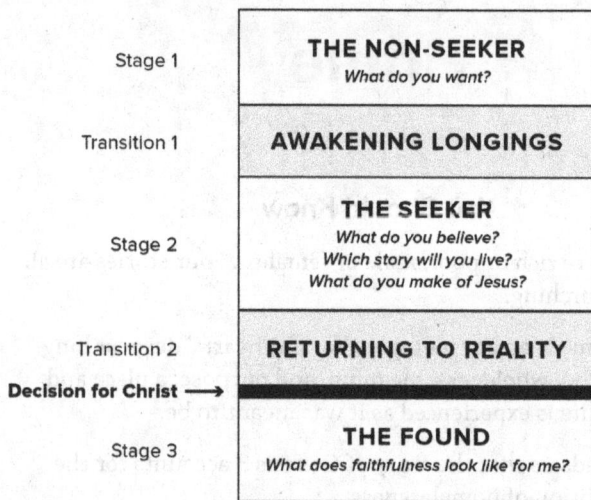

| Stage 1 | **THE NON-SEEKER**<br>*What do you want?* |
|---|---|
| Transition 1 | **AWAKENING LONGINGS** |
| Stage 2 | **THE SEEKER**<br>*What do you believe?*<br>*Which story will you live?*<br>*What do you make of Jesus?* |
| Transition 2 | **RETURNING TO REALITY** |
| Decision for Christ → | |
| Stage 3 | **THE FOUND**<br>*What does faithfulness look like for me?* |

**FIGURE 8.1 THE JOURNEY HOME**

## Essay Questions

### Short

1. The metaphor of the "home" we long for includes a sense of meaning and purpose. Briefly describe your search for this aspect of home. How have you understood and pursued a sense of meaning and purpose in the past? How do you understand your sense of meaning and purpose now and in the future? (p. 203)

2. Briefly explain the stories of naturalism and postmodernism. Do they seem implausible to you, and why or why not?

3. What is "Ministry in Four Dimensions"? Explain, using examples. Why is the fourth dimension important?

## Long

1. What is home to you? Explain the multi-faceted account of "home," and then describe in some detail the particular elements that make up your longing for home.

## Quiz

1. What is the broad outline of the "story of the world"?

    a) Paradise — fall — redemption
    b) Home — away — home again
    c) Orientation — disorientation — reorientation
    d) Entitlement — loss — gratitude

2. Which of the following is NOT an aspect of "home"?

    a) The place where you belong
    b) The place where you are fully known
    c) The place where your purpose is discovered
    d) The place where your every desire is fulfilled

3. (T/F) According to Gould, home is both a place and a path.

4. Self-reliant attempts to "find our way home" fail because _____.

    a) They don't correctly diagnose our fundamental problem
    b) We get distracted from the quest for happiness
    c) They aim at the wrong worldly goods
    d) The number of goods we need is too great

5. Which of the following is NOT an aspect of the paradox of life in Christ?

    a) We die in order to live.
    b) We seek another to find ourselves.
    c) We find our way outwardly by looking inwardly.
    d) We gain the whole world but lose our soul.

6. According to naturalism, humanity's fundamental problem is _____.

    a) Physical discomfort
    b) Survival in a hostile environment

c) Discord between people groups

d) Ignorance of the world

7. Why, in the postmodern story, do we individually and collectively lust after power?

a) Because power brings with it great pleasure

b) Because power allows us to control the resources necessary for survival

c) Because power allows us to define what is true

d) Because power makes us like God

8. How does the fundamental problem of oppression get resolved in the postmodern story?

a) By revolutionary overthrow of the oppressor

b) By the oppressed telling their own stories

c) By discovering a single unifying story that everyone accepts

d) By a revelatory awakening of the oppressors to their evil

9. According to Frederick Buechner, what makes the Christian story a comedy?

a) That God's rescue was unforeseeable

b) That the Bible illustrates God's sense of humor

c) That the story has a happy ending

d) That the plotline makes us laugh with joy

10. The primary question the cultural apologist asks of the non-seeker is, _____

a) What do you believe?

b) What do you make of Jesus Christ?

c) Where are you going?

d) What do you want?

**Notes**

www.ingramcontent.com/pod-product-compliance
Lightning Source LLC
Chambersburg PA
CBHW011746020426
42331CB00014B/3298